HORIZONS

HORIZONS

THE ROYAL AIR FORCE IN THE TWENTY-FIRST CENTURY

GEOFFREY LEE

FOREWORD BY SIR RICHARD EVANS CBE

Published in 2005 by
Ad Hoc Publications
Cedars, Wattisham Road, Ringshall, Suffolk IP14 2HX, England
www.adhocpublications.com

ISBN 0 946958 45 9

Edited, designed and typeset by Roger Chesneau

Printed in England by The Lavenham Press

Contents

Foreword

Sir Richard Evans CBE

I am very pleased to have been invited to provide the Foreword for this impressive book. As a former Chairman of BAe Systems, I took particular interest in the air-to-air photographic achievements of British Aerospace photographer: Geoffrey Lee.

Geoffrey, now a director of Planefocus Ltd, is universally recognised as one of the world's leading air-to-air cameramen. He has been involved in over 500 air-to-air sorties across all seven continents and has flown in more than a dozen military fast jet aircraft types. His acclaimed photographs have appeared across the front covers of all of the world's major defence and aerospace magazines and, in addition, they have featured in countless books and television documentaries. This year he celebrates twenty-five years' flying experience—a fantastic achievement and one vividly portrayed in the pages that follow.

Geoffrey's photographs—which show Royal Air Force fixed-wing aircraft of all varieties from the Tucano trainer to the Hercules transport, from the faithful Canberra to the ubiquitous Tornado and from the Vigilant powered glider to the very latest Typhoon—are a tribute to the skills and dedication of the men and women of the RAF. The images capture the technological achievements of the modern British aerospace industry and the latter's continuing role as a world leader; they also highlight the continuing vital importance of the armed services and of the defence industry in a constantly changing world.

This luxuriously produced, high-quality book—which comes with the promise of a future, companion volume depicting the Royal Air Force in the 1980s and 1990s—is a truly unique study of military aircraft at work. I commend it to you.

Preface

If anyone had told me when I joined Hawker Siddeley as a photographic apprentice thirty years ago that I would in due course fly with the Royal Air Force and travel the world, I would have been amazed. Over the years, however, I have been fortunate enough to photograph every type of aircraft in the Royal Air Force, from the Spitfire to the Eurofighter Typhoon. I have worked with many squadrons, and with the most talented aircrews in the world, and along the way have made lasting friendships. What more could one ask of one's work? Now I am delighted to have been invited to produce a published record of some of it.

This year, 2005, I celebrate a twenty-five year association with fast-jet, air-to-air photography. I still feel an adrenalin rush with every sortie; I still enjoy the challenge of finding new techniques to capture images of aircraft being put through their paces by consummate professionals. I work with fantastic people and thrive on their comradeship. We all get a real 'buzz' when, as a team, we achieve that 'how-did-you-do-that?' image. I can truly say that I love my job..

The photographs presented here are but the tip of an iceberg, beneath which are expert flight crews, engineers and technicians, all of whom have a proud commitment to achieve excellence. The images are the result of meticulous planning, thorough crew briefing, immense concentration by all, absolute discipline, immaculate timing, good weather, trust and, finally, a little luck. Ninety per cent of a sortie is preparation and ten per cent achieving the goal. There is no room for error, nor for repeats: the team must get it right first time.

Technically, I rely on my camera kit to perform perfectly, despite relentless stress and g-forces. My Hasselblad 500 ELM and 500CM with 80mm, 50mm and 38mm super-wide lenses have been the loyal servants of my trade and deliver unbeatably crisp, accurate images. For weapons-release sorties I have used the Nikon F4 and F5 with 35–70mm zoom lenses, and in recent years, responding to the digital age, I have introduced into my repertoire the Nikon D2X digital camera using the 17–35mm lens, and this also produces excellent results.

My work cannot be conducted without a great deal of support, and this book would not of course have been possible without that support. I am indebted to all the Royal Air Force squadrons and flight crews, past and present, who have invited me to join them and have continued to fly me over the years. For this volume, I would especially like to thank Nos II (AC), IV (AC), 10, XI, XIII, 14, XVI (R), XVII, XIX (R), 20, 29, 31, 39, XLI (F), 47, LIV, 72 (R), 99, 100, 101, 111, CCVII (R), 208 (R), 216 and 617 Squadrons, the Central Flying School, the Battle of Britain Memorial Flight and the Royal Air Force Aerobatic Team (The Red Arrows). No 100 Squadron, who have repeatedly welcomed me to their sorties, deserve an extra word of acknowledgement. My thanks go also to countless people in BAe Systems for their assistance over the years, and in this connection I would specifically like to mention Sir Richard Evans for very generously contributing the Foreword for this book. Finally, my gratitude is extended to my loyal and long-suffering family, particularly my wife Melanie and my parents Bill and Muriel, for their unwavering encouragement and belief.

Thank you all.

Geoffrey Lee
Camberley, Surrey, July 2005

Toucan Tango

Tucanos of Nos 72 (R) and CCVII (R) Squadrons

The Tucano is the Royal Air Force's basic flying training aircraft, entering service in 1989. Nos 72 (R) and CCVII (R) Squadrons, featured in these photographs, are based at RAF Linton-on-Ouse in Yorkshire.

294
ZF294
BASUTO
447
ZF447

417
ZF 417

417
ZF 417

These photographs were taken over Yorkshire in April 2004 from a No 72 (R) Squadron Tucano.

447
ZF447
447
294
ZF294
294

Cause for Alarm

A Tornado F.3 up from Leeming

DG
ZE763

A weapons load of two MBDA ALARM, four MBDA ASRAAM, two drop tanks, an acquisition pod and a BOZ pod characterise this Tornado F.3 from No XI Squadron based at RAF Leeming.

DG

DG

ALARM (Air-Launched Anti-Radiation Missile) is the RAF's standard anti-radar weapon and first saw service in the Gulf War; ASRAAM (Advanced Short-Range Air-to-Air Missile) is the standard air interception weapon, replacing Sidewinder. The Swedish-designed BOZ pod is a countermeasures dispenser.

Black Hawk Up

One Hundred Squadron; one hundred years

No 100 Squadron's XX313 was photographed on 3 April 2003 wearing a 'zap' commemorating the one hundredth anniversary of the Wright Brothers' first powered flight at Kitty Hawk.

YEARS OF FLIGHT
XX313

RESCUE FROM EITHER SIDE
FLT LT HARVEY

These photographs also show Flight Lieutenant D. Harvey (above) practising his display sequence for the 2003 season. His Squadron is based at RAF Leeming in Yorkshire.

XX313
CE

The Hawk is one of the most successful military aircraft of the modern era, with over 900 built or on order for nineteen different armed services. While essentially a training aircraft, it is a more than capable light combat jet too. Most of the images in this book were taken by the author while flying in a Hawk of No 100 Squadron.

CD
XX278

CD
XX278

Photographic Finale

Last orders for a faithful servant

The venerable Canberra has served the RAF in a plethora of guises since 1951 and a handful are still in service, operated by No 39 Squadron (No 1 Photographic Reconnaissance Unit). However, current (2005) plans envisage the aircraft's being withdrawn in 2006.

XH134
AA
XH134

XH134
AA

Tornado Ninety

A celebration by No 14 Squadron

1915-2005
BX

No 14 Squadron's anniversary aircraft, Tornado GR.4 ZG756/'BX', is pictured here with the MBDA Storm Shadow missile system. The aircraft is being flown by Flight Lieutenant Paul 'Zig' Froome and Squadron Leader Rob Barrett and is based at RAF Lossiemouth.

As well as No 14 Squadron, RAF Lossiemouth is home to three other Tornado attack squadrons—Nos 12, XV (R) and 617.

1915-2005
BX

1915-2005
BX

Ab Initio

A Vigilant powered glider from RAF Syerston

This Grob G.109B Vigilant T.1 powered glider is from the Air Cadet Central Gliding School based at Syerston in Nottinghamshire. In the photograph opposite it is seen overflying RAF College Cranwell.

ZH 247
AIR CADETS

AIR CADETS
ZH 247

Maverick Harrier

A tank-buster from No IV (AC) Squadron

This Harrier GR.7 has a weapons load of Maverick rockets and gun pods, together with a pair of drop tanks. The aircraft is from No IV (AC) Squadron based at RAF Cottesmore in Rutland.

The Maverick is an IIR-guided 'fire-and-forget' anti-armour missile. These photographs were taken in September 2001 from a Harrier T.10 of No IV (AC) Squadron soon after the weapon entered service with the RAF.

Fire and Brimstone

No 31 Squadron gets new teeth

Tornado GR.4s from No 31 Squadron each armed with twelve MBDA Brimstone, four MBDA ALARM, two drop tanks and BOZ and ECM pods. Brimstone is a long-range, 'stand-off' anti-armour missile developed from the US AGM-114 Hellfire.

DK
DH

No 31 Squadron are the first to receive the MBDA Brimstone and to fly their Tornados with this new weapon fit.

No 31 Squadron Tornado GR.4s are based at RAF Marham in Norfolk. The photographic sortie for these images took place in January 2005.

DH

Hawks One Two Three

On manoeuvres with Nos XIX (R) and 208 (R)

339
XX339
339

158
XX158

Here two No XIX (R) Squadron singletons, one with a centreline gun pod and wing-mounted CBLS (Carrier, Bomb, Light Store) and the other with underwing Sidewinders, are put through their paces . . .

. . . and here a 'clean machine' from No 208 Squadron joins the sortie, overflying the magnificent scenery of North Wales.

185
XX185
339
XX339

No XIX (R) and 208 (R) Squadron Hawks are based at RAF Valley on the Isle of Anglesey.

Overleaf: Three Hawks from No 208 (R) Squadron in immaculate formation over a stunning backdrop of mountains and cwms.

174
XX174
183
XX183
185
XX185

TriStar Tanking

Topping up with Two-One-Six

The RAF's TriStar KC.1s are operated by No 216 Squadron as both air-to-air refuelling tankers and troop transports. They are based at Brize Norton. Here two Tornados from No XIII Squadron get replenishment.

ROYAL AIR FORCE

ROYAL AIR FORCE
ZD953

Here a flock of No IV (AC) Squadron Harriers gathers around the TriStar. The Harrier's refuelling probe is situated on the left main intake, conveniently just behind the pilot's shoulder. It is both retractable and removable.

Cats Get Fitter

Jaguars escort a Polish Su-22

Two Jaguars from No XLI (F) Squadron based at RAF Coltishall, Norfolk, photographed over East Anglia in the company of a Polish Air Force Su-22 on an exchange detachment.

9616
FP

The camera-ship for this sortie—which took place on 20 August 2004—was a No 100 Squadron Hawk from RAF Leeming. The Su-22 is from 7. Eskadra Lotnictwa Taktycznego, 33. Baza Lotnicza (7th Tactical Aviation Squadron, 33rd Air Base).

9616
FP
FA

The flat, agricultural, East Anglian landscape stretches out as the jets make their way to RAF Coltishall, depicted at far right. The camouflage paintwork on the Russian-designed Sukhoi looks effective against this type of terrain.

9616

7309

Eagles Volante

On the wing with No XI Squadron

WN

Sky Flash (underbelly) and Sidewinder (wing-mounted) have for many years been the standard air interception armament of the Tornado F.3, as shown on this aircraft from No XI Squadron.

No XI Squadron is one of several dedicated to the Air Defence of the United Kingdom. The Squadron is based at RAF Leeming in Yorkshire

Storm Brewing

The Typhoon enters service

Typhoons from No XVII and No 29 Squadrons in formation en route to the RAF Leuchars air show in September 2004.

BH

The Typhoon supersonic 'swing fighter'—in production by the four partner nations of Great Britain, Germany, Italy and Spain—is now entering service with the Royal Air Force, gradually supplanting Jaguars and Tornado F.3s.

No XVII Squadron functions as the Operational Evaluation Unit and No 29 as the Operational Conversion Unit, both smoothing the introduction of the Typhoon into RAF service.

BH
XXX
FS D J MICHAELS
SQN LDR D A FELLOWES
XXX
XXX

Over 600 Typhoons are on order for the four partner nations' air forces, and Austria and Greece have also made commitments to purchase.

SQN LDR D A FELLOWES
FS D J MICHAELS
XXX
XXX

BE
XXX
XXX XXX
ZJ806

Heavy Haulage

No 99 Squadron's big lifters

ZZ173
ROYAL AIR FORCE

CR
XX335

The Royal Air Force operates four C-17 Globemasters, all leased from Boeing. They are assigned to No 99 Squadron at RAF Brize Norton.

ROYAL AIR FORCE
ZZ173

The C-17 is the largest aircraft operated by the RAF, its dimensions—174ft long, 170ft wingspan—marginally exceeding those of the TriStar KC.1

ROYAL AIR FORCE
ZZ173
ZZ173

Simply the Best

Aerial artistry by the Red Arrows

ROYAL AIR FORCE

Perfect symmetry: the Red Arrows—the Royal Air Force Aerobatic Team—practise their routine, mid-season, June 2004.

The aircraft are seen here over their Lincolnshire base, RAF Scampton, and the surrounding countryside. The photograph below shows the 'Big Vixen' formation.

ROYAL AIR FORCE
ROYAL AIR FORCE

Red Arrows aircraft are virtually identical to the standard Hawk trainers seen elswhere in this book but have a 70-gallon tank under the centreline containing diesel oil and dye for making their famous coloured smoke.

Multi-Role Mixture

All the squadrons from RAF Marham

These images show four Tornado GR.4s—one each from Nos II (AC), IX (B), XIII and 31 Squadrons—plus a Canberra PR.9 from No 39 Squadron, all based at RAF Marham in Norfolk.

These photographs were taken over the East Anglian coastline in November 2002 from a No 100 Squadron Hawk based at RAF Leeming.

AL
F

Facta non Verba

No 20 Squadron spits fire

33

The photographs here and overleaf were taken over the Holbeach firing range and depict Harrier GR.7s of No 20 Squadron (based at RAF Wittering, Cambridgeshire) practising with the CRV-7 rocket system. This weapon is carried in underwing pods each containing seventeen units; various warheads are available, but a typical fit is a 10lb HEAT (high-explosive, armour-piercing) round.

36
ZD407
36
ZD407

Jaguar Ninety

Nos XVI (R) and LIV Squadrons sign off

Nos XVI (R) and LIV Squadron Jaguars in their eye-catching special paint schemes, 21 February 2005. The Squadrons were established in February 1915 and May 1916, respectively.

90
Years
1915-2005

90
Years
1915-2005
1916-2005
54(F)
XZ112

These photographs were taken from a Jaguar T.2 of No 6 Squadron a few weeks before Nos XVI (R) and LIV Squadrons disbanded.

90
Years
1915-2005
1916-2005
54(F)
XZ112

Treble-One Tribute

A special Tornado F.3

This is a No 111 Squadron Tornado F.3 in a special paint scheme to celebrate the unit's 85th anniversary. The photographs were taken in September 2002 close to the Squadron's base at RAF Leuchars.

UV

The aircraft is carrying four MBDA ASRAAMs but no underbelly medium-range missiles. The lightning flash on the forward fuselage recalls Treble-One's long association with the English Electric/BAC Lightning interceptor in the 1960s and 1970s .

1917 2002
ZE159
UV
UV

1917-2002
UV
ZE159

Trainer Treat

A No CCVII (R) Squadron Tucano shows its paces

A Tucano of No CCVII (R) Squadron—up from its home base, RAF Linton-on-Ouse, Yorkshire— is seen here practising its routine before the start of the 2005 flying display season.

294

294
ZF294
294

294
ZF294
294

294
294
ZF294
294

Hawk and Herky

No 47 Squadron gets an escort

CQ
XX351

The Hercules is the RAF's transport 'workhorse' and has been in service for some forty years. This particular aircraft is one of the early variants, identifiable by the four-bladed propellers. 'Affiliation flying'—dummy interceptions—involving the Hawk and the Hercules is regularly practised: despite its size, the Hercules makes a difficult gunnery target, thanks to its superb manoeuvrability at low speeds.

209

Storm Shadow

No 617 Squadron displays its new missile

This Tornado GR.4, from No 617 Squadron, based at RAF Lossiemouth in Morayshire, is equipped with a pair of MBDA Storm Shadow stand-off missiles, carried under the aircraft's fuselage. Storm Shadow, a long-range cruise missile with a highly penetrative capability, is of rectangular cross-section and, once launched, deploys wings for stability in flight. It was introduced to service in the RAF by the Squadron in 2002 and was employed operationally in Iraq the following year. It can also be carried by the Harrier and the Typhoon.

No 617 Squadron is of course the famous 'Dam Busters' unit of World War II fame; its legendary exploits are commemorated in the tail emblems of its aircraft.

AJP

AJ·P
1943
2003

VC Tanking

Tornados and Harriers take a 'prod'

Like its TriStars, the RAF's VC-10s are converted airliners and are capable of both air-to-air refuelling and passenger transport duties. The fuselage fuelling point identifies the variant dispensing to the No XIII Squadron Tornado as one of the later (and larger) VC-10s in RAF service, this No 101 Squadron version being a K.4. Amongst other variants of the aircraft, the RAF also operates the slightly less capable (and smaller) VC-10 C.1K, and the No IV Squadron Harriers are refuelling from a No 10 Squadron tanker/transport of this type.

ROYAL AIR FORCE
XV109
11
ZD330
62

On the Prowl

Up and about with No XLI (F) Squadron's Recce Cats

After equipping the RAF for over a quarter of a century, the Jaguar is now being withdrawn from service. One of the last squadrons on type, No XLI (F), is featured here, its aircraft carrying 1,000lb bombs on the underfuselage rack. 'Foxtrot Papa' also has an overwing Sidewinder acquisition round.

FR
FK
FF

FR
FK
FF
Anniversary
XZ398

In 2001 No XLI (F) Squadron celebrated its 85th anniversary and marked the occasion in a modest way by decorating the fin of one of its aircraft, as seen opposite. The incongruous colours on the drop tanks of three of the aircraft are a hangover from the green/grey camouflage scheme of the 1970s and 1980s. The Squadron's 'Foxtrot Mike' (overleaf) is carrying a Vinten electro-optical reconnaissance pod on the centreline station.

Lest We Forget

A Lancaster accompaniment

Some two dozen Lancaster bombers survive around the world but only two are airworthy, one of which is the famous PA474, currently in the markings carried during the war by EE161 of No LXI Squadron. The aircraft, which forms part of the RAF's Battle of Britain Memorial Flight, continues to delight the public with regular appearances at air shows. She is shown here accompanied by Hawks of No 100 Squadron.

QR M
M
CQ
XX351
CN
XX314

QR M